LION THOUGHTS VOLUME 1

by Samuel

Life is complex. Life is simple.

Copyright @2018 by Samuel Bagot

All rights reserved. This book or any portion thereof may not be reproduced or used in any manner whatsoever without the express written permission of the publisher except for the use of brief quotations in a book review.

First Printing, 2022

ISBN-13:   978-1-7331102-2-8

ISBN-10:   1-7331102-2-4

www.TheWakingLion.com

The true alpha doesn't necessarily confront others,

but the true alpha must confront themself.

- Samuel

Contents

The Thing That Is 1

The Inner Structure 17

The Refuge of the Soul 45

The Spiral 58

Origin Of Morality 76

Why I Fight..82

The Power of Self-Actualization 94

Why I Write..101

Be Brave! 105

The Thing That Is

We don't know who we are, and we're born into a place where we can't explain our arrival. We make up ideas that fill the gaps to carry on, but ultimately, we don't know why we're here. We find ourselves in a place where we are born without our knowing consent. There is a history that we are taught that attempts to inform us of our past, but our only option in this place is to call things as we see them in the present. With that hazy form of discernment, we are here making decisions and just surviving. Religion comes into play in our journey at some point. People, governments, and control structures come into play as well. We are caught in the middle of all these circumstances, and life is confusing.

God nowadays is more or less forgotten in the mainstream public experience. That all-knowing being, that many believe we're a part of, is gone from our mainstream reality. While it's impossible to say what God is, it's important to think about. Old concepts from religions and legends try to inform us of what God is. There's Zeus. There's judgmental guy in the sky. There's mother nature. There's the spaghetti monster.

Religions like Jedi and other designer religions exist which suggest that God is a force of some kind.

But what is it really? What is that concept at its core, and why was it so heavily believed in the past. Why was it such a strong part of the past civilizations and cultures but is just gone now from modernity? Even atheists attempt to explain existence during their denial of purpose. Atheism is more or less just another religion of believing that we're just here by science, rocks float in outer space, and we're bags of chemicals. There are lots of definitions and attention paid to explaining our existence from many directions. Each school of thought attempts to define what God is, but they all seem hazy for some reason.

When I open my eyes, I see a thing in front of me. It's ever present. It's the world. It's life. It's people, conversations, and time. This thing is omniscient in nature. It encompasses all energies and flows in a specific direction. It's beautiful. It's both happiness and sorrow.

If you take a toaster oven and break it apart. It will be pieces, and each piece has a name. When you take those pieces and put them together, they make a toaster oven. Then you call it a toaster oven. If you break it in half, it becomes two halves of a toaster oven. But really, it's just a bunch of stuff. It's just a bunch of matter. The term toaster oven, springs, and power cord are just names that we give things so that we can talk to each other about them. We sometimes categorize things based on their use. You can use it to toast stuff like bread. You can also use a toaster oven as a hammer, right? You can use it as a paper weight. But we call it a toaster oven because we use it to toast bread, and that's what it's built for.

Anyway, my point is that a toaster oven is lots of things. It's a collection of individual things that in aggregate make up one thing depending on how we look at it. But in the end, it's actually just a collection of matter. The pieces of the toaster oven can be thought of in aggregate as one thing when they work in concert. Thinking on, this toaster thing has that same relationship with the table it sits on. There's the table, and there's a toaster oven. But they can be viewed as a single thing. They are just two different parts. When you put the toaster oven on the table, it can be said to be a new singular object called a "toaster station."

The toaster station is now one thing in our minds. Every "thing", any object that we would call a thing, actually has that relationship to whatever is around it. Transitively and intrinsically, everything has that relationship with every other thing in existence no matter their distance apart. This relationship is held between all things in existence, and by definition, all things can be seen as the same singular thing. The plane flying through the air is, in this way, the same thing as the fish swimming in the sea. They are the same thing when moving in concert.

The sun rises, and in comes the day. It goes overhead. The sun sets, and the night starts. We see the moon. Then the sun comes up again, and it's a day. It goes away, and it's a night. Then it's a day. Then it's a night. But really, the sun is always somewhere, and it's day there. Day and night are just aspects of our view. We label it day and night, but they are actually constant and work in concert in one motion. The day and night working in concert was here before us, and is just one long day in the end. There is no real separation between the days. You just like to sleep in the dark. And I don't blame you. I do too.

It's all really one long day, right? It's all the same day. It's just time. It's just this place. Our conversations are that way too. You wake up in the morning, and there is no one there. You talk to your dog, and, of course, I'm talking about myself now, right? You talk to your dog, and you fix some breakfast. You go to work, and you listen to the radio as you talk to yourself while you're going to work. Who were you talking to that whole time?

You get to work, and you say hi to someone in the kitchen. You talk about what you're going to do that day and what you're lining up in some project. That's a conversation with someone in the kitchen.

Then you walk to your desk. While you're hanging out on your own typing, someone else walks up to your desk. They start talking to you about something else. They may say, "We have this thing to do, and what do you think if we did..." That's a different conversation, right? But you think about a common thread of things in between all these conversations. The ideas you think about in between the conversations pertain to those conversations. You take information, stances, and emotions from one conversation to the next, and you mill them over in your head in between consciously or sub-consciously. Thoughts bleed from each conversation into the following conversations. These conversations seem to flow like this throughout each day.

When it comes down to it, like day and night cycling, all the conversations throughout the day are the same conversation in your mind. It's was just one long conversation for the day. And as all of the days are the same day, all the conversations where just one long conversation. Life, as we call it, is not a collection of conversations, concepts, and ideas you pieced together. It is actually just one long conversation. Your entire life and the conversation that you had with yourself is a singular experience. The world that you found yourself in is a time and space for you to have the experience of that conversation. I hope you enjoy it.

That's what I see in life. It's just one long day. It's just one long conversation. It's a conversation you have with yourself in this place which I call The Green Gift. The conversation ultimately isn't with any specific person. It's actually with that singular thing which is all things moving in concert. There is only one thing. It all melts together without the definitions. It encompasses much more than we could hope to envision. It's all the same thing. There is one object in existence, and it includes the green gift you found yourself in. I'm not trying to be pedantic or overly meta. There are important lessons to learn from simple observations.

Everything from the trees, the flowers, the breeze, the camera, the conversations, the people, and the days are all just one thing. It's a force of energy that's just there, and we don't know where it came from. We don't know what it is. But we were born into it inside of its image and with some of its characteristics. We are born into this. And here we are. We don't know what it is, and, as a part of it, we don't know what we are.

We can trace back our family lineage to some degree. We can trace some science suggesting we were hominids at some point that we branched off evolutionarily. We can hypothesize about the points in time where we were just single celled organisms. But our view gets hazier and hazier the further back we look.

Closer to home, you may know about your mom's life, but you know less about your grandparent's life.

Most people don't know anything about their great grandparents, and almost no one knows anything about their great-great grandparents. If you go back a couple more generations, it's just darkness and void. We literally don't know where we came from. You don't know your family line. You don't remember lots of your childhood either. We don't know human history past a certain point, and most of what we do know is revisionist history and fake. We can't even get yesterday right anymore. If you turn on the news to any channel, you will see talking heads lying about what happened 30 minutes ago. What makes you think that your history books are accurate about things that happened 1200 years ago?

So, we are constantly in this state of not knowing where we are, and this experience is too large for us to see or understand. It's just a motion of energy that's turning and moving. It's not to be known. It's not to be understood. This thing, being all things moving in concert as a singular thing, I refer to with a proper noun, "The Thing". There are things like a cantaloupe, the camera, your dog, and the sun. So, there are things, but then there is "The Thing." Capital T; The Thing. The whole Thing that is moving and churning. That concept is what I feel to be monotheism. It's the difference between thinking that there are separate things and that there is just one thing. And that Thing is God. That thing, which includes you, is God. This is monotheism.

This view of the nature of our experience is true for all living creatures. It's also a concept that is religion-less. Religions seems to chase this concept, and we know it to be true in some capacity. It's a concept that many religions have in common, even the atheists. Some religions embody this better than other religions, of course. Religions are found in books, rituals, traditions, and there is a dogma to them. That's because people seeing something complex want to place road signs so that others will take note as they walk the path. They want to pass down helpful ideas from generation to generation. In that cycle, the observations of The Thing That Is naturally turn into religion in a cycle of dogma wrestling with the divine.

I don't think there is anything wrong with religious structure, and I actually feel it's important. Humans have a deep symbiotic relationship with our religions. We identify with rituals and traditions. We use them as tools to teach our children to ultimately seek the spiritual though they may not understand in their youth.

We're on a path that others before us have walked, and we actually can't make it without listening to what those before have immortalized in testament. It is, however, up to every individual to seek deeply enough to realize that it's all the same thing and look towards what brought us here. When seeking that which Is and ultimate truth, lots of our ancient rituals and text make more sense. Seek and you will find. The Thing That Is brought us here, and It is our creator and father.

The Thing That Is includes everything that "is" and everything that is true. It specifically excludes everything that "is not" and everything that is not true. Truth is our only sanctuary and we are clearly commanded to never replace The Thing That Is with a false reality. Everything outside of What Is is mental illness, sorrow, and death. Optionally, once we journey through enough pain, we learn to seek out the father and return home where we, as newly risen warriors, clear the lies and live in peace with family.

There are those that hate What Is and they create a darkness that pushes against What Is. The nature of this darkness and evil is very simple. The darkness moves closer as a slow, deliberate removal of all the protective, truthful ideas that protect you and your mind. The darkness replaces then truth with mental illness and ideas that are intended to eradicate you and your family. It is the nothingness. There is no greater example of the darkness than the modern media which are consistently fraudulent. The darkness inevitably reveals itself as a demand to alter the breeding pattern that produces life.

I was born and raised Jewish, but I was raised in the country. I didn't have a strong connection to Jewish or Christian teachings. I wasn't exposed to what the root of Judaism really was. I did attend a bit of temple when I was young though. Being raised in America, there's a lot of Christian culture, so I saw a lot of Christianity as I grew up. Earlier in my life, I didn't understand any of the core concepts being talked about by the Christians or Jews. Other people seemed to be into it for some reason, and that seemed nice to me.

I wasn't raised with a religious orthodoxy or any sort of fear of what would happen if I didn't act a certain way. I was very free in my thoughts and explored the world freestyle. But in all my experiences, I did catch wind of this concept that everything is the same thing.

I also saw clearly that there is a right direction to walk, and we don't get to choose that direction.

I always got a strong sense that the Green Gift and The Thing That Is were meant to be observed. I have always felt like there was something miraculous and veiled just beyond our limited sight that is designed for us to seek and find. Buddha taught this and the rarity of life. He taught self-reflection. All of this, I felt from a very young age, and I think others feel it too. It's something learned throughout life even without heavy guidance from religious structure. But the lack of guidance makes a very rocky road which can be terrible because sorrow and mental illness can spread like mold.

Later life, I read religious text like the Torah and the Bible. They make a lot of sense to me now, and I see hints of that miraculous Thing that was always waiting just outside my sight. I see an ancient guidance explaining that there is a right path to walk. The text also say that we don't get to choose that path and sorrow is the price of pride. It's not a coincidence. Our religious roots make sense, and I see I'm not the first person that has walked this path. Our traditions chase the eternal and help us on the path.

For instance, I focus on The Thing That Is. Then later in life, I read:

> Moses asked God, "Suppose I go to the Israelites and say to them, 'The God of your fathers has sent me to you,' and they ask me, 'What is His name?' What should I tell them?" God said to Moses, "I AM WHO I AM. This is what you are to say to the Israelites: 'I AM has sent me to you.'" God also told Moses, "Say to the Israelites, 'The LORD, the God of your fathers—the God of Abraham, the God of Isaac, and the God of Jacob—has sent me to you.' This is My name forever, and this is how I am to be remembered in every generation....

When God was asked what he was in the testament, he responded with a phrase and not a label. He said something along the lines of "I am what I am" which is a common English translation of the Hebrew phrase "אֶהְיֶה אֲשֶׁר אֶהְיֶה" or "ehyeh 'ăšer 'ehyeh." Other translates of this Hebrew phrase include "I am who I am", "I will become what I choose to become", "I am that I am", "I will be what I will be", "I create what(ever) I create", or "I am the Existing One". My addition, which I didn't know fit when I adopted it from my dream research, is "The Thing That Is."

There are concepts that you can think of that are fantasies. And then there is a concrete Thing that is in front of you. That Thing that is front of you IS, and it alone shows you truth. It IS. It is The Thing That IS. And there is nothing else. Being dishonest or deceived as to what that Thing is only brings sorrow by definition because a person who is lying to themselves is then operating off of assumptions that are not. Sorrow is just confusion of operating off of assumptions that are not true and not functionally in tune with reality.

Pride is the origin of sorrow. There are lots of things that we hear about, talk about, and think about that just are NOT. They are false narratives. These specific ideas are just not true. Sometimes we convince ourselves of these false ideas. We sometimes think that we can bend the concrete direction of life towards our will. In these situations, we are operating as if we can choose What Is true, and this is pride. While moving in pride, we are simply walking away from what is true and into painful lessons. This can be referred to as walking away from the Thing That Is. Society asks us to lie a lot about what is true in life such as the purpose of sex and the purpose of men and women.

Evil forces compel us to lie to ourselves about the obvious dangers to our families evolving right before our eyes in this modern world. One of the biggest lies is that power over other men doesn't corrupt. Some even lie and say there is someone out there in the dominance hierarchy of man that will represent you and look out for you. The dominance hierarchy that man builds does not provide for you or look out for your family because it's an aggressive pyramid scheme of flawed men and agendas. It's a tower with fatal flaws that inevitably crashes down. Abandon the dominance hierarchy of man in your mind as soon as you can.

We can see many of the weak people around us completely drowning in lies that they tell themselves. The main characteristic of modern society is mental illness. It's an eyesore. We are approaching a point where you can be attacked or even killed for being someone who isn't lying to themselves. Fear of personal physical harm is a compelling factor in many people's capitulation to the darkness. Fear is the motivator of weak men. I don't know much, but I can promise you one thing. Walking away from discernment and what protects your family, The Thing That Is, brings more sorrow than any threat from a man or government.

There are lessons of people's walk away from truth in any given testament. It really is amazing. The "I Am" is a recuring theme in our path towards resolve and tranquility for a reason. Interestingly, we are given free will to ultimately choose The Thing That Is instead of our own way of pride. We are born here, and we don't know what we are. It brought us here to experience that observation as self-reflection. We can't say exactly what The Thing That Is is, but that doesn't matter in the end because we simply know It Is.

Hopefully you think this is interesting. If you want to see more reflections on The Thing That Is, read some more of my thoughts, and see where it pops up. All glory goes to The Thing That Is. And don't forget...

To Wake the Lion!

The Inner Structure

What is the spiritual structure behind our thoughts? What is life? Without an underlying inner structure to life, a species experiences first death, the beautiful ones arrive, and then it experiences second death. Don't worry, I'll explain. We'll also go through how this is relates to our physiological approach to fulfillment, belonging, family, and link all of it to the human orgasm.

In general, when we talk about life, people generally think of breathing, blood pumping, brain signal activity, and vitality in a physical sense. But in someone's eyes, if you look deep enough, you can see something else as far as the presence of life. Life in general, is a force of energy moving through a generational pattern and through time and space. That is to say that life is a recurring loop of beings from one generation to the next and a movement of beings that replicate off of each other. They multiply throughout time and space to create a branching tree, The Tree of Life. The pattern of that tree branching becomes visible as living beings replicate based off the generation before.

So, when you see life in someone, you can very much directly associate a person with the phenomenon that brought them not only into life physically and vitally, but also the phenomena historically and psychologically that brought their exact branch of The Tree into existence in the present. People aren't simply individuals but dually a growing Tree branch that hopefully will go and branch in other directions and keep the energy flowing. The drive of mankind is to keep The Tree burning. Some Tree branches, of course, do not continue, and this in ways can be considered to be selected against the by what people call evolution and what some call reality, etc. It is the Tree of Life, and we are the branches and leaves of that Tree.

When you look in someone's eyes, don't just notice that their heart is beating, their eyes focus, and their lungs are breathing. Look deeper into their mind to see what it is that may or may not drive them to create another successful generation. And when you see that they're vital, also take into consideration if they are strong enough in their life force to create another successful generation in the face of the adversity which every generation and every living being encounters naturally in the course of existence.

Objectively for this conversation, by another successful generation, I mean being capable of producing the next generation and being able to have more generations after that. Success would be passing on a cyclical mentality that doesn't contain detrimental mental flaws that would cause future generations lack of the resolve to survive. Success means the thought patterns of the parents and children do not set up the blood line or species up for extinction. Simply breeding is not a sign of a successful new generation.

There's a lot of resource type physical adversity as far as overcoming obstacles and gathering the resources to have and protect a family. These are a natural part, and the easier part, of a human's struggle to exist throughout time and space. That part is the physical support life needs, and while important, there is another part in our minds and behaviors that is required to support life in our hearts and minds, the Inner Structure of Life. This other aspect of the struggle can be illusive in that it's hidden, unlike the physical requirements of life.

This other hidden aspect includes mental, spiritual, and/or psychological attributes which are referred to here as the Inner Structure supporting life.

It's somewhat of an inside skeletal structure to the flesh that travels through time and space. A good metaphor would be, when people are building skyscrapers and large buildings that reach into the sky, they first build a steel frame. The steel frame is like the skeleton inside of the building. The frame is built from floor to floor, and it's the underlying, structural rigid piece of that building which provides the support and integrity. This steel frame is basically the sole factor in its long-term longevity on earth. All of the concrete floors, windows, ceiling tiles, bricks, and even all of the desks and tables sit on this steel frame. The steel frame is the skeleton of the building.

So, when we look at life on earth, the steel frame is the psychology of producing a strong child and another generation that is strong enough to survive earth's adversities. The Inner Structure is not only in the parents' minds, but also must be passed to the child's mind, and also passed to all of the generations of minds forward. That Inner Structure actually transcends generations and reaches from generation to generation and itself spans time. The psychology spans time in our thoughts and conversations in parallel to our flesh spanning time. This Inner Structure travels through time and through every human. The Tree is both flesh and thought.

It isn't a different similar Inner Structure in the minds of each generation, but the same Inner Structure handed from generation to generation. The energy of these thoughts transcends us, travels through us, and through The Tree. It's like a lightning bolt that passed through time and space, and as it does this, flesh grows in person shaped manifestations along its path. It's the illusive energy that is being refereed to when we're reminded that a man can't live on bread alone. We must love, respect, and pronounce our gratitude and commitment to The Tree and this radiating energy. It persists even after the death of an individual and carries on into the future. This Inner Structure compels and waters the Tree of Life and is ultimately indescribable. But I'm going to try to describe it anyway, because that's what I was told to do. More practically, the inner structure is what we are referring to when we use nebulous words like spirituality and psychology.

So, what is it to be alive? What is life? It seems accurate and attuned with reality to say that life is not simply when your heart is beating and life is not simply when your brain is firing. Life actually is only thriving when an individual's heart is beating and they have the psychology and underlying mental structure to focus on creating the best next generation that they can create. And by best, again, I mean specifically a generation that will have another successful generation and will carry on life. The experience and presence of Life is the goal of Life. By definition, a person is thriving less if they do not try their best to compel life and to carry on another generation. There is something listless about disliking children. Life in ways is not just the beating heart, and to be alive you have to do more than beat your heart.

In the 40s, John Calhoun did a series of experiments where he placed rats inside of a big rat paradise cage and gave them unlimited resources so that they could breed to maximum capacity. He wanted to observe their behavior when physical limitations where nullified and their internal mental resilience was challenged. And in the timeline towards maximum capacity, he observed how the rats behaved socially. It turned out that the rats for one reason or another slowly gave up on their ability to act as rats, which he basically defined as having natural breeding patterns and taking care of children. That is of course an obvious baseline for the health of a civilization. This baseline of health included the female rats taking care of the children and the male rats also defending their nests and gathering resources. These are known natural, intrinsic gender roles. When the population grew to the point where there was too much social interaction and not enough room to raise children privately, for some arguable reason, they abandon the basic gender roles for which they were biologically designed. Females no longer took care of their young and the males no longer defended their nests. The smaller males stopped eating and wouldn't defend against attacks from larger males. Some of the males retreated into corners where they continuously, neurotically groomed themselves and no longer engaged in breeding. These were called "The Beautiful Ones." They had no concept of the next generation. The females, of course, were constantly being harassed and endless mating attempts on them made them psychotic. They were mentally broken and abandon their children. Also, the males, having no chance to act on the normal gratification of their biological gender roles, became unstable, violent, and even engage in cannibalism of the children.

A rat population that reached this point was never found to be recoverable in any way experimentally. At an observable point in time, the minds of the population collectively shattered. The point at which the minds shattered was referred to as the "behavioral sync". The point at which there was no more reason to exist. There would be no more family. There would be no more happiness or fulfillment. Rat populations experiencing the behavioral sync consistently spiraled to complete extinction. Any rat exposed to a behavioral sync event could not recover even if separated from the mentally ill population and placed in a fully healthy, thriving population. That rat's Inner Structure was broken forever.

Calhoun referred to the behavioral sync and shattering of the minds as "First Death" because there was no chance of recovery. The subsequent physical death he referred to as "Second Death". Second death is also a biblical term from Revelations 2:11. Life is more fragile than we understand and isn't right. Isn't guaranteed, and must be fought be fought for when threatened.

The point of all this is that despite any hypotheses of this type of behavior occurred in the rats, at a certain point, the rats abandoned their familial breeding pattern and their ancestral knowledge. Their ancestral knowledge was a chain of thoughts which had been built in them for millions of years through evolutionary adaptation, parental communication, and dimorphic sexual selection evolution. Dimorphic meaning two forms, male and female. They abandon their ability to produce the next generation successfully.

There was no way that the next generation could look to their parents to see how to behave in order to produce another generation themselves. If one generation is skipped, that branch of The Tree wilts or dies. You are a castle in the sand. Once the rats' social order and gender roles were broken, they had no reason to continue attempts to cooperate or to have any sort of interest in the next generation. They no longer behave like rats, and lots of them just stood there frozen and catatonic. There was no reason to act in any way for any reason. Calhoun also referred to time of the behavioral sync as Hell.

Once the Inner Structure was shattered and gone, the rat's bodies with beating hearts and firing brain cells were pointless. Even with infinite physical resources, there is still a requirement for an underlying mental Inner Structure to see the gift of life and carry life on as a breeding pattern that produces successful generations of Life. The Tree of Life does not exist without the underlying assumption that there will be more branches and more leaves. The Tree of Life is the master plan. The Tree is the only plan. Without its underlying Inner Structure holding up our day to day hopes and dreams, the Tree wilts and we wilt within. A curse on all of our houses and on I for winking at your discord. But I won't accept this and neither will you.

Wake up, stand up. The time is coming when simply passing by will no longer suffice.

It's said by very wise people that man does not survive on bread alone. And what does that mean? We can see that there is a set of understood non-negotiable, physical requirements like eating and sleeping. You'll die without them. Less understood, is a set of invisible, non-negotiable mental requirements like seeing children in a certain light and knowing not to steal. Life that does not push to produce more life ends, so there's a requirement intrinsically thereof that life love life. That's one of the non-negotiable mental requirements for life to continue. There are, of course, others.

Bread represents a physical need, and man cannot survive on bread alone. I love life more than my own, and I don't just want it to continue. I'm going to personally make sure that Life continues against all odds.

A person cannot simply live life and enjoy life without the internal fundamental notion that it should continue. That person needs to have a direct plan and adopt it as their purpose. If you feel like your life has no purpose, this is your infinite well. This is a gold mine with infinite gold. All-purpose must in a deep way be formulated out of loving life and wanting more life on earth with gratitude for The Tree. If you talk to people about gratitude, you'll see this notion sift out, and if hit the right notes, you can see it in their eyes. My postulation is that gratitude for being here and wanting more life is the root of and only purpose in life. And is can be flavorfully masked into a multitude of Earth's intriguing pursuits and hobbies. It is a requirement for life to continue. I think that this is why ancient texts talk about praising What Is so much. What Is as a proper noun alluding to God.

    We're compelled to look around us and appreciate the beauty in life like the trees and sunrise. And while that may seem obvious, why do we feel that way and where does that feeling come from? We are told by others and in all basic narratives to appreciate each other and to be happy and fruitful. The drive of life does exist inside us and for it to exist it must require that we be grateful enough of life to endure the sacrifices of the pain that life entails. Sacrifice is required as life isn't free, and that time comes for all of us. And while life is a force that's so mysterious that we can never fathom its movement, we personified it somehow by picturing it wanting us or demanding we worship it or that we give it all available glory. What Is is the only thing to be praised and no false idols can replace it.

The Inner Structure is beyond our comprehension because it's ancestral in nature all the way back to humanity's creation. This world is how we experience the underlying inner structure of life that flows through generations. That Inner Structure spanning generations manifests in our emotional pattern as awe and loyalty to the Tree of life.

These concepts are very basic and axiomatic in nature and potentially seem obvious. Going through the motions of talking about them is important because we must decide on a strong stance towards the basic nature of life so that more complex stances in life can be made with solidarity and resolve.

The Inner Structure compels a path towards the continuation of life through our emotions. This is why a child being born is basically the most powerful moment of existence. It's also why a father dancing with his daughter at her wedding is such a powerful moment.

It's why your children's piano recitals are emotionally engulfing. It's why a beautiful woman's image is so intoxicating. Its why men are willing to rush a beach into oncoming machine gun fire in order to make a better world where their children can survive. It's why I flower smells so sweet. It's why you can watch bumblebees on a flower, and it be so intriguing yet so simple. You'll never see something more basic, yet amazing, than a bumblebee gathering pollen to take back to its family. You'll also never be able to fathom the complexity of what's going on in that exact moment of why that bee is gathering pollen. All the interesting events listed above can be felt in your chest. These emotions are hormonal and the structure and triggers for those hormones are visibly written on each strand of DNA in your body. You can't control it. It's just what you are. Because It is what It is.

You'll never be able to fathom how long the bees have been gathering pollen and why they decide to operate from generation to generation. They love their children like you love yours because The Tree makes beings in Its image.

Millions of years we've been here. We've been doing this for millions of years though we've change shapes, we change names, we developed these languages, we flew into outer space, and we charted the galaxy. Yet we still do the exact same basic psychological loop where we seek the next generation. And the next generation is the most beautiful part of anyone's life. And the birth of your children is a moment of thousand times more powerful than the best promotion you've ever got at work. The thing that guides us deeply within is an Inner Structure, and it's actually very simple. It's related to the experience of the continuation of the Tree of Life.

Fulfillment comes from gratitude and loyalty to that Tree, and there is a difference between fulfillment and happiness. This phenomenon is talked about a lot in every society and every culture throughout time. There's always been the danger of confusing happiness and fulfillment. Happiness is something that occurs in the moment and more or less seems to coincide with a temporal effect of some event that occurred. Basically, it's temporal and fleeting. Fulfillment is when one can look back on their life and know that they fulfilled their purpose. If one is to be fulfilled and content in life, they must find how the Tree and purpose are related.

One thing that can harm our personal fulfillment is damage to the traditional family structure. One way to decay the traditional family structure is with confusion brought on from misplaced sexual energy. Sexual energy is a gift we have to share and is the attractive force between men and women as they create life. Casual sex is sex without keeping our purpose within the Tree of Life in mind. Misplaced sexual energy is an attempt at temporal happiness at the cost of long-term fulfillment.

We see this manifest in our lives as sex can be used to produce the most important moments in life such as having a child and making a loving family. Sex can also be used without reference to the Tree of Life where it becomes an addiction and a cruel master that only reminds a person of their deeply seeded loneliness in this world. There is nothing more depressing than only being able to have sex with people that don't care about you. And we were never told that. No one talked to us about family structure in this way when we were young adults. We are the product of an abused generation in that way, and it's our job to fix now. We do what we must because we can.

Children and family are Tree oriented. Causal sex self-oriented. We don't currently teach our children and young adults this basic nature of sex anymore, and they suffer most of their lives with the confusion and loneliness of being dragged through a secular, hookup culture. This was our parent's fault, but it's our fault now, and it is our problem to fix. By that, I mean it's your fault personally, and you are directly responsible in ways that you fully understand. We do this to the kids and it was done to us through trashy, state sponsored public education, Hollywood, and ridiculous talk about sexual revolutions. None of it was true. We were lied to. And on the brink of the death of our species, that is glaringly apparent.

We sent the next generation into the dark thinking that this low level of concern for their future was normal. It's not normal. Hookup culture and plan B dates are not normal. You shouldn't need to be on birth control to have a social life or find someone who will care about you. It's a sickness. It's a mental illness. We are sick. And that sickness is warping you and it's warping your children. Wake up! It's ok to take a strong stance on this. Take a strong stance on this. You will find that people will support you in ways wouldn't have imagined. Most people agree with this, and people who respect life, family, and gender roles are in the overwhelming majority in America and on Earth. Don't let any bully you.

When I was younger, I asked a man in a store how he had gotten such a good deal on a computer he bought for 70% off. His response was "Because I'm strong, and I don't let people push me around." He said it with a straight face and he meant it. It amazed me. I had never thought to feeling that way about myself before. It blew my mind for years to come. Don't let people bully you. They're weak, and we are strong.

Of course, sexual energy produces arousal, which is needed. Sexual arousal and is strongly related to the neurology of the orgasm. And the orgasm is a great example of a temporary happiness, but has the option of resulting in a long-term fulfillment. Biologically, the origin of the orgasm is that an animal will seek out a very strong pleasure response through mating. The reward is a heavy dopamine and oxytocin chemical release in the brain which we call an orgasm.

Put simply, less socially structured animals, as well as humans, seek out the orgasm because it feels good. But in the case of humans, we are more structured and can choose when to have orgasms and if they will result in a child. So, we have the option to use the orgasm for fulfillment or for selfishness. We have the option to completely abandon the next generation of humans if we decide and that's what many people do. That choice is not observant of the Tree and these people are not capable of achieving the higher levels of fulfillment like seeing their children in piano recitals and father daughter dancing at weddings. They ultimately are confined to shallower modes of existence and often develop a distain for themselves, the world, and life itself.

Less socially structured animals like deer and antelope seek the orgasm and inadvertently another generation is born and they don't have a knowing choice. They don't understand the link between the orgasm and fulfilling their purpose. They just know that the orgasm feels good and they seek it out. Inadvertently, they also, according to their gender roles, know that they have to take care of the child. Fulfillment for them is just being what they are naturally and watching life unfold. This I refer to as "walking with What Is". They may or may not link the orgasm and the child, but it all works out because they don't use their minds to build an alternate social structure to nature that separates the orgasm from their purpose within the Tree of life. The assumption that we can or will build a better, alternate social structure is called pride. It's the origin of the death of species.

So, humans are socially structured enough to where we can separate the orgasm from the creation of a child. This is a dangerous evolutionary situation that we've arrived at. The development of an advanced species attempting a higher consciousness will, by simple math, inevitably reveal the point in the development of that species at which they have to respect the more complicated inner workings of their own minds. They will reveal the point in time when they must show that they can handle their mind proactively and maturely in order to survive. They must realize that they can actually decouple the orgasm and child birth, and bring about their own death. And they must avoid that separation if they are to survive. Nietzsche spoke of stepping away from the natural order while trying to convince ourselves that What Is is dead or that God is dead.

Upon coming to the point where we can separate the orgasm and child birth, we have to realize that we shouldn't. The orgasm is the natural order of producing the child. It is beautiful and a gift from the Tree. Man cannot create another system or as Nietzsche said "kill God" to create our own moral set in any way that we could handle appropriately or successfully. God is not dead. We are the variable in the equation.

Inevitably every species will get to that point, and humanity is at that point right now. We are being given the choice to make up our own nature and will certainly fail, or to admit to ourselves that we are not in control of anything and there is a higher order to what's going on.

We WILL admit that there is a higher order to what's going on in nature, and except that there is a spiritual morality where we yield to the Inner Structure that compels the Tree of life. We WILL NOT re-wire the brain and mind after hundreds of millions of years of evolutionary sexual selection. To think we have that power or capability is hubris and can only produce sorrow because life requires a strong next generation. The Inner Structure of life that has spanned generations since our inception is there specifically to help and guide us through the complex time that we're experiencing now. Our faith cuts through confusion like lightning cuts through the night sky. At this point in our evolution, we are to decide the nature of sex and value of our family structure.

We are given the choice slowly as we become more intelligent to decide what we want and the question is always, will you decide your own way, or will you be still and accept What Is? Will you walk with What Is? What Is wants the orgasm to be a bonding moment between two people who are about to build a strong family link. Our neurology is built through generations for that and is based off that.

We, as a naturally more intelligent species sexually select based off of aspects of the mind such as intelligence, integrity, and family values. Part of that selection is choosing who you give that spiritual orgasm to and who you make that bond with. When we decouple the orgasm and the bond, we end up with all kinds of seeking and seeking of that orgasm, but more rarely produce a next-generation. Or equally degenerative, a child may be produced without a strong Inner Structure transfer which is a derelict and harmful to the child. Any interaction that produces an orgasm for temporal gratification is a miss and has no value towards the greater human destiny. A more steadfast utilization is choosing who you have an orgasm with because you want a next-generation and are grateful for the gift of life and want it to continue. When you're solid and you want to raise that next-generation with solidarity, purpose and fulfillment are produced.

This is why lots of the text say not to have sex before marriage. It's not the plan to have sex with people that you don't plan on having kids with. Of course, these are all considered to be archaic viewpoints, but turns out to be true. We aren't taught these aspects of life by our parents anymore, but we will return to these more realistic understandings as we learn from the degradation of our society and species. Not recognizing the purpose of the orgasm and what it did for us evolutionary is actually wilting our branch of the Tree of Life. We have strayed from what we really are and our next generation is on the cliff. Evil does exist as a constant counter measure to the Tree of Life and resolves those branches of the Tree that don't fulfil the requirements of continuing life. It resolves those branches by dissolving them. The orgasm is spiritual in nature and is very important.

We are inundated with strange types of psychologies towards sex and relationships in our modern society. This is why, to some degree, it's getting harder for advanced civilizations throughout the world to carry on their breeding patterns and to carry on strong generational continuity. Many of the strongest nations, like Japan, are crashing in their population production. In the UK, lots of the natural national UK women don't want kids and the population is decreasing. These are all symptoms of modernity and mental illness. In America, we have population problems as well. Family structure being broken down and the presence of the father is declining.

Modern children are showing record amounts of psychological, behavioral, and emotional issues. Many kids raised in this modern psychopathy basically can't build meaningful relationships or find a mate. Modern kids can be extremely emotional and unable to handle even minor stressors. Many, if not most, college aged Americans show significant mental illness and psychotic emotional and behavioral problems due to loneliness and purposelessness. Currently each generation has less mental integrity than the previous and is more susceptible blaming others for their problems and victimhood mentalities. And their children will be even weaker than they are. We put our next generations on a cliff by lying to ourselves about the basic nature of life and reality. Family creates stable children and there is no substitute for that.

This mimics the rat experiments. A civilization got so advanced with near unlimited resources. When it came to the point that the rats needed to take their intelligence and combine it with spiritual awareness to get through that next evolutionary gate, they faltered and fell apart. They couldn't carry through with solid familial roles and their minds shattered under the stress. They couldn't produce another generation, their population crashed, and could not be returned. We are seeing that decision point now in our species. We are being threatened with first death, but we will overcome where the rats failed. We have divine tools that they didn't have.

But when will the exact point come? I think we approach it quickly, but even if you disagree, you at least have to realize that we will get to the point of the test inevitably. It's a math thing. It's coming. Look around at the modern breeding patterns, attacks on family structure, and psychological and sexual attacks on our children and realize that we're at least close enough to start pushing back on the evil that preys on us.

Life is amazing and an overwhelming majority of people are very happy to be here. Remember, we are the majority. Life is beautiful and people innately seek it. It's as simple as the ancient texts said. Stop questioning everything and just be with What Is. We don't make it up, and our constant attempts to redesign everything are just a neurosis. When we mess with the basic nature of our elation, orgasms, family structure, etc., it fails and causes sorrow. It's the story of the apple, and we can't say we weren't warned.

We will realize the glory of What Is and the gift that we've been given. And we follow what makes us feel the most fulfilled, which is taking care of our kids and producing solidarity for our children and family structure. That is to listen to and foster the Inner Structure of our minds which we didn't create and is our gift to pass on to the next generation. They won't live happy lives without it and that inner tranquility is the most important thing above all else to teach to children. Morality trumps education and family trumps career. The nasalism of the nothingness is always watching but can't stop our drive to fight for our families and children.

This is the only way to long term happiness and the only path that pans out into fulfillment. This is the path to our greater human destiny, and all other paths end in extinction. Drinking beer, smoking weed, having sex with people outside of the family structure, pursuing career goals instead of family, etc. are all temporary attempts at happiness that do not thrive in the Tree of Life. To carry on, we must pay attention and give the proper gratitude to the Inner Structure of life, the beauty of generations, the relationship of the orgasm to family, and playing our roles though we don't understand them fully. These actions produce fulfillment and are gifts that What Is gave us. And that's actually as simple as it really needs to be.

When we have respect for life, we properly and maturely handle the orgasm. When understanding the relationship pattern between the children, the woman/, and the man, we create a strong family structure. The man, the woman, and the child become an emotionally geometric construct that I call the Triad. Like a stone arch is a structurally unparalleled physical formation, the triad is an unparalleled speciological formation. They are both geometric in nature. In the big picture, the Triad is the atomic element of the most powerful force in existence. This force, in motion, is the carrying of the Inner Structure of life throughout our generational species and throughout time and space. This most power force, is the force of life itself, the Tree of Life. The tree that burns yet is never consumed.

You want a solution to the world's problems? Be still and know What Is. It has it covered and has told us how to survive our problems. I just think it's beautiful and I would like to express my gratitude for the whole thing. I try not to take orgasms for granted or take women for granted. The bigger picture is the deepest meaning a human can experience. The love of someone of the opposite sex. The love between man and women is timeless and beautiful beyond our ability to understand. It physically produces a child also beyond our comprehension. I couldn't imagine a greater hope than for everyone to seek and experience life. No other action, series of events, social situation, or alignment of civilization could possibly reach the eclipsing fulfillment of the alignment of the Triad.

The Triad is the building block of life on earth and geometrically supports the branches of the Tree of Life. Because our minds are evolutionarily hormonally based, the Tree is the source of 100% of the beauty that you see around you. The beauty you see in life is the radiating nature of the Tree. The Tree that burns yet is never consumed. Our emotions burn inside us and drive us towards survival and gratitude for What Is. Don't seek your own truth. Foster the Inner Structure of Life, and seek What Is to be a part of the Tree. All glory goes to God.

Thank you for watching and thank you for being a part of my life! If you think this was at all interesting, give me some feedback. Like and subscribe. And don't forget...

To Wake the Lion!

The Refuge of the Soul

Life's a storm. It's very difficult. It's not always easy to find shelter in this place. Very little works out, and it never lets up. Life never gets easier. It only gets more difficult. The thing that makes it all worth it is that the rewards become greater and greater as you move through life, and when things are lined up properly, the good easily outweighs the bad. That's our gift, and the world really is our oyster.

When you're a kid you have no responsibilities and relationships are easy. Homework is your worst problem, and you meet new friends every day. You have no debt, and everything is free. As a kid, you don't notice the most important thing that compels your day-to-day happiness, which is your family. You get that for free too.

As you get older, friends become more difficult to meet, and your responsibilities start to become numerous. At a certain point, you become aware that your big picture goals and your fulfillment is being tested by hard times. You notice your goals require serious diligence to actualize which only complicates the now mounting difficulties in your life. You start to give up on fair weather friends as you start to concentrate on the few people you feel give you support and value. You realize that it's no one's job to support you or be there for you. It's just a fact of life that everyone is just taking care of their own life and doesn't owe you anything. In the end, basically no one really cares about you in the way you need, except for possibly your family. That is, if you're lucky and it was lined up right.

Then at a certain point, the original pillars of your support system, like family and childhood friends, start to fade away. The big pillars die off. Your grandparents pass on, and then your parents pass on. This is the slow peeling back of your original free support system, and you must then replace it with a support system that you create on your own. Christmas used to be tons of parents, uncles, and aunts, right? If you want that big family Christmases again, it's no longer free. You must make that family.

You must then create a support system that is primarily or solely built of family if you want to every feel home again. It will be a new family as an extension of your original family. Then you can have those big

Passover meals again. Then you can have those warm Thanksgiving meals again. Only then will Christmas feel like Christmas again. Those people will care about you and need you the way that no one else could. It's no one else's job. As your original support system fades, you must make your own anew from scratch... physically. You literally must make your own family and a place where you belong by becoming whole and creating a it. Then you teach the kids to do the same.

I completely understand how obvious this stuff is when you hear it out loud, and that's my point. It's obvious, yet no one ever sat us down and talked to us about how hard life would become. They didn't tell us how to find shelter in the storm. The family is the refuge of the Soul. The family unit has all the larger fulfilling events that make life worth it and keep the good times out-weighing the bad. And trust me, the good times can easily outweigh the bad.

Some examples of fulfilling, high-note moments would be events like seeing your child be born, watching your son's piano recital, opening Christmas gifts with 20 other family members, family vacations, family movie night, eating dinner with loved ones every night, watching your daughter get married, the father/bride dance, meeting your grandchildren, and simply having a place where you belong in this world.

Those feelings and journeys don't just happen for free like we assumed when we were kids. They must be created, and there's a path that must be followed to hit those high notes. Basically, all the greatest moments offered to us are on the path of family. Within the promise of modernity and progress, we're not shown that path. It's hidden from us, yet it's the most important path. Many people find later in life that they're left out in the storm. The rain never stops, but it could've been much easier for them.

Modern society leads the children astray. In the story "Pinocchio", the children grow donkey ears and become slaves after being lured off to focus on fun and avoiding responsibility. Abusive figures lead them astray by convincing the children to make bad decisions, and we lead our children astray by not telling them what's import in life. It's highly important to seek shelter from loneliness and nasalism.

Family is the refuge of the Soul! Pinocchio's friend, who dies as an enslaved donkey, has the name of Lucignolo which ironically sounds like the modern term YOLO. It's a coincidence though and actually it translates to Lampwick. Go back and watch Pinocchio again after you finish this conversation and you'll see this message. His father is the only one that cared about him in the end. Pinocchio father always wanted a son and needed a child to fulfill his life. None of this is new.

Why were we never talked to about this? It's one of the most important of all lessons. Family and blood line are unrivaled in importance. Why is this not taught in schools from a very young age. In ways, it's a combination of laziness and nasalism which have possessed the parents of the world. They avoid this most basic of lessons to their children because the lesson wasn't given to them. Like any cycle of abuse, they were abused by careless subscribers to modernity, and they pass that abusive reality as normality to their children. I also see a great evil in the world that hates beauty and fights against the Tree of life. This most valuable of lessons is that evil's Acylase heel.

If we just focus on the lesson of family, and we will, we'll push back the darkness into the night for a thousand more years and be at peace again. The turmoil in the world is directly related to the distance and cold space inside the family unit. Family is really all you have, and heaven really isn't that far away. You'll learn that in one way or another as you move through life and the later you learn that, the more likely you'll be eaten by the nothingness.

I'll tell you one thing that helped me learn. Daphne was born on April 27, 2012. Her full name is Daphne Eleanor Bagot Von Slippy-Slop Pancake Face 2012 Edition. She's my best friend. When I got her, she was smaller than a cantaloupe! She was fat and her head was shaped funny. I took her to work every day, and she slept in my lap hidden under my desk. When she got too big, she laid across my feet all day at the office and kept them warm. I watched every movie with her and held her like a teddy bear for almost 2890 days.

I had a motorcycle accident which broken my leg, and I couldn't walk for about three months. She laid beside me the entire 3 months while basically none of my friends visited me. And since then, all those friends faded away. When I was sick, she was there. When I was lonely, she was there. When I would come home drunk, she kept me warm. It's like she knew I was drunk. She'd meet me at the door at 3am. She taught me how to love, how to be selfless, and how to depend on someone else. I don't think I knew how to love someone before her. I had never seen that before I don't think.

She's a character, and her favorite thing is wearing her pink sweater and walking through Home Depot to beg for treats. She was a ruthless, dirty, rotten beggar. She was the softest thing ever, and the demeaner in her eyes was that of a child mixed with an elder sage. She was the warmer of worlds, and a stealer of bacon. I didn't know what tense to put this writing in, but I figured it would work itself out. She was a fancy fawn boxer canine. I love you, Daphne Eleanor!

I thought she would live a long time, and it really didn't cross my mind that she would ever go. Or I assumed at lease she would be maybe 10 or 12 when her time came. She won't be making it to her 8th birthday though. I took her to the doctor about a month ago because her leg was hurt, and they informed me that she had late-stage lung cancer, and she wouldn't be making it much more than 4 or 5 months. 11 medications and 3 chemo therapies later, it turns out that the cancer was much more powerful than we thought, and she's quickly winding down after only a month and a half. She's coughing more and more, and she's drifting away. You need to understand that you'll go through this in your life. Your friends don't care. Your coworkers don't care. Politicians don't care. Only your family can care about you the way you need when it comes down to it.

I'm keeping it together because it hasn't really hit me yet. I was pretty sad when I first heard, but a person can't be catatonic for months on end and that would be a pretty sad last time with her. So, I just got over it and vowed to fight it with her. We've hung out a lot, and the time has been great as it always is. But it's going to completely wreck my life when she is gone. With her dies my whole crew and all of my friends. Basically no one knows me anymore and probably hasn't for over a decade or more now. There are pretty much only acquaintances at this point. Don't worry about me though, I have a secret and I'll be fine. But it still sucks. Don't hang your only hat on a moving train car.

Don't get me wrong, I'm the biggest dog person you know. I will always have a dog or two. I'm seeing in our experiment with modernity, people attempt to replace family with dogs and cats. People refer to their dogs as their children in an obvious attempt to mimic a divine purpose in life. People get multiple cats so as they die, they can cycle through them without gaps in emotional support. They talk to their pets like humans because it's our nature to express ourselves and be understood. I do lots of that kind of stuff too by the way. But when they turn to gold and fly away as they are called, you need to have placed bigger rocks in the river to step onto next.

     People try and replace the need for a family in all kind of ways like having drinking friends and drug buddies. They drink every weekend because it creates a façade of a group of people that is there for us with some consistency. Some people focus on careers where coworkers and hierarchy mimics family structure and belonging, but can ultimately drive them from having that role in a real family. They seek validation from work status and coworkers. Street gang recruitment is based highly off of offering lost children family structure. In all kinds of ways people waste valuable years that they could have been a part of something real.

     Here is the point of all this. We live in a very isolated world, or lots of us do. I don't know how it got to this point, but it's just not right. You never hear about the isolation, but it's uncanny and rampant. We fill our time with socialization, work, and floating from one setting to another. We have very quaint private lives that most of us spend alone. We're heavily encouraged to focus on aspects of life other than family, and often we end up with no one understanding us or caring about us.

I love Daphne, I don't know if I would even be here without her, but pets are made to be our companions and teach us love, but they are fleeting. I think this is why they only last about 10 years. If they lived as long as us, we could recluse into their hearts and be content until our passing. But the Tree of Life doesn't work like that. Dogs teach us how to love and have supportive relationships, and then that new understanding MUST be executed and applied to a family unit or you'll simply find yourself standing back out in the storm. You don't belong in the storm alone.

Pets are amazing family members, but can't replace family. The human branch of the Tree of Life wouldn't grow if we didn't have to deal with each other, which is much more difficult that a pet. A girl would have left me a lot time ago for coming home drunk like that. We need to encourage children and younger people that family is the most important aspect of their emotion wellbeing and long-term fulfillment. We leave them to find that out on their own in their 30s far past an immense amount of loneliness and mistakes.

That's modernity in a nutshell. It's catastrophic and breeds nasalism. Yet, this is called progress. How Orwellian. We should be teaching children to value and seek the stability of a family unit at a much younger age. We would be much better off as a species if we had a society where people sought the shelter of family anywhere from 18 to 22. Or at least before 25.

We teach children the avoidance of family for the sake of school and careers, which is even worse of an idea than trying to replace a family with cats. Lots of people out there were taught that an office cubical can replace your child hugging your leg, and that taking care of yourself when you're sick is great cause you're challenging the norm. And no one told them any differently. Now they're in their late 20s and 30s, and they're alone. No one cares about them. Do you want that for children?

Our society marches these people through public education, through college, into a career, into a cubical, and never tells them that it won't make them happy. Family is more valuable than career and personal achievement. If you've never been told that and told to focus on building your family, then no one ever cared about you in that way. And that's wrong. It's abusive to push a child through a machine and into a cubical. If you understand what I'm talking about then you must understand, you are a product of nasalism. It's a generational degradation and I say enough with it.

We're going to fix it with the gift we were given. It's ok, all we have to do is break the cycle and move back towards more family-oriented public conversation. We must talk to the children about what's truly important in life. We must break the cycle and in ways admit that modernity can't replace our basic imperatives. Take the love you learned from your pet and apply it to a real human that needs it as soon as possible. Sober up and start a family. And if you can't have kids, find someone who wants to adopt and build a later stage family to be a shelter for a lost child... and you. Family is the refuge of the soul.

Remember the true Alpha doesn't necessarily confront others, the true Alpha confronts himself or herself. Thank you for watching and thank you for being a part of my life! If you think this was at all interesting, give me some feedback and read some of my other pieces. Like and subscribe. And don't forget...

                                                            To Wake the Lion!

The Spiral

Life is a spiral of two forces. The two forces that make up reality are the masculine and the feminine. These energies spin around each other in a motion to create children, to expand life, and to offer the experience and enjoyment of the Green Gift. These two energies are polar and incomplete. They seek resolve in each other like magnets spinning around each other. In physics, this phenomenon is referred to as charge valence. They come together and complete each other. This phenomenon is a duality in that it is both physical and spiritual/emotional, which I'll explain. This combination of energies is dually the biological systems which produce life and the spiritual/emotional systems we refer to a as security and fulfillment. It's a dual occurrence of the physical and spiritual. These two forces physically and emotionally actuate the desires of the sexually selective evolution inside sexually dimorphic species. I'll explain more and hopefully make this clearer. This conversation is about understanding us as humans and the way our minds work.

We, along with many other species, travel through time via sexual replication. We have offspring that carry on into the future as we individually pass away. Species which traverse time through sexual replication are biologically sexually dimorphic. "Dimorphic" means two forms. This means that they are binary, and the human's two forms are called male and female with specific chromosomal configurations for each. Humans DNA contains 23 pairs of chromosomes and each chromosome pair has one contributed chromosome from the mother and one contributed chromosome from the father. 22 of the chromosome pairs determine solely physical characteristics. The 23rd chromosome pair is called the sex chromosome and determines the sex of the fertilized egg and offspring. Male sex chromosome configuration is noted as XY and Female chromosome configuration is noted as XX. Other sex chromosome patterns exist but are disordered, highly infertile, and not included inside the mechanism of sexual selection reproduction. They are not part of this conversation. For the purposes of this conversation, when I say chromosomal pattern, I'm talking about the configuration of the sex chromosome because this conversation is about sexual selection evolution and the binary nature of life. This conversation is about the two energy forms that originate from the two forms of sex chromosome expression which are XX and XY.

We travel through time by accruing genetic adaptations inside our DNA's genetic code if those adaptations help us adapt and survive inside the Green Gift. The Green Gift being this world we were offered. Our genetic code travels inside of us and we carry it with us in the nucleus of each one of our cells. We are the vessels that carry the genetic code through time. In the course of a genetic code traveling through time, it travels through the many generations of a species, like us humans. In its travel, the genetic code replicates itself in two ways. A lot through cells multiplying as a being grows and a little through the being making cells to breed like sperm and eggs.

Personal cellular growth is the normal growth of a being as it ages. We as individuals get physically larger and we get heavier. Our cells multiply. During this process, the DNA strand doesn't change and stays stable for the most part simply replicating cells. There's some other stuff to note here like the phenomena of X inactivation, but I'm going to keep it a little simpler here. The future of the DNA expression does not experience any significant changes or recombination during this time. During this process, the DNA strand is traveling through time with no change. This time I'm referring to is the life of the creature. DNA is stable throughout the life of a creature and doesn't change.

In sexually dimorphic species, a fertilization process occurs to create a new life and a new being. This is the breeding process in transition from one generation to the next. During this fertilization process, the future of the genetic DNA code does experience a change and recombination. The fertilization process is a genetic recombination which produces a new and different DNA combination from either of the contributing parents' DNA. Even more interesting is the fact that, after the fertilization process, the resulting fertilized egg's DNA set is a universally unique set of DNA which has never occurred before in history anywhere on Earth or throughout existence. Its uniqueness includes all of time back to the big bang.

Though each of the fertile sexual participants has two sex chromosomes like the XX and XY pattern, the two combining sex chromosomes that go into a fertilized egg are each just one of the parent's full pairs of sex chromosome. The male has a sex chromosome pair of XY and will contribute only one of his two chromosomes which will either be an X or a Y chromosome. The female has a sex chromosome pair of XX and will contribute only one of her two X chromosomes. They will each contribute one of their two sex chromosomes in this way to make a full pair for the fertilized egg. A cell carrying only half pairs of chromosomes is referred to as haploid cell (meaning half). A cell carrying full pairs of chromosomes is called diploid (meaning whole). Sperm and egg cells are examples of haploid cells, and your fully formed cells like your heart and skin cells are diploid. A fertilized egg is a diploid cell and the first in the chain of cells of a new being entering the Green Gift.

In humans, the male contributes a haploid cell with a copy of either his X or his Y sex chromosome, and the female contributes a haploid cell with a copy of either her X or her other X sex chromosome. The male haploid cell is called a sperm, and the female haploid cell is called an egg. The produced diploid cell is called a fertilized egg and is a new set of DNA. As I stated before, the fertilized egg is a new set of DNA chromosomes and the new creature will have a combination of the contributing parents physical and mental features. And keep in mind that the mental features are a product of the physical features of the brain, so the mental features, like optimism and aggression, are also physically derived and coded in the DNA. We all know that the apple doesn't fall far from the tree.

While there is quite a bit of misinformed conversation and debate over when life begins, life is actually never begun or ended. The male was "alive", contributed a "live" sperm cell to a "live" egg from a "live" female. The combination of the two created a "live" fertilized egg. This new egg now has its own new, unique DNA strands and immediately begins cellular replication to produce more "live" cells. Those live cells are a "live" zygote and fetus, and the produced born baby is also "alive." Life doesn't start at fertilization. Life is a continuous motion of "live" cells which carry out all the cellular level processes of life individually. Each cell lives out its own adventure and life span. Life doesn't start at fertilization, it started millions and millions of years ago and never stopped. It's a continuous chain of DNA replication and "living" cells tumbling through time. This is the Tree of Life and its millions of years old or more, and so are you.

Life pulls you in many different directions. Social, political, and other obligations... We're constantly looking for the solutions to the world's problems. But these problems we see are all abstractions of the base forces in life which are the resolve to breed, see the life we were given replicate, and watch it grow from birth towards consciousness as we did on our path towards our destiny. To give something the Green Gift as we were given and protect it as it experiences life. This is the true drive of mankind and of all sexually dimorphic creatures. The course of our destiny is to travel through the world, find ourselves in the same place we started, and recognize it for the first time.

Everything in our lives from buying coffee, to finding a job, to cutting the grass ultimately serves our need to compel the next generation. Some is more direct like smiling at a girl, and some is less direct like setting up a 401k. However, it's all to server and expand the Tree of Life and a larger plan of our Genesis that we could never fathom.

Our base form is this ancient chain of cellular proliferation traveling through time as a Tree of Life. It's actually the thing passing through time and we act out it's confrontations with the physical world as individuals. We are really just contributing to its confrontation with the inanimate physical world. The Tree of Life is animate and the basis of the physical universe is inanimate. The miracle of Life is to turn the inanimate into the animate and create life from non-life. The miracle of G-d is to literally makes something out of nothing. It is self-actualizing in this physical plane and that's why our self-actualization is so important to us as individuals. The Tree animates the lifeless world like a plant's roots digging into the soil. It's growth in our respect, requires birth of children which explains why all of our genetic code is code for breeding. It never dies, and it's older than the Sun. You are older than the Sun.

The Tree requires that you be bold in the solutions to your problems because while you may think them difficult and numerous, you were given the spark of divinity. The love for your children and mate is evolutionary in that it compels you to never give up. You are designed to never know exactly why you must carry on, yet also designed to feel that everything rests on your choices and that you must do the right thing. Do you feel that? That feeling is accident and is written in the DNA of each one of your cells. It was in the egg with you when you became fertilized and could be traced back to the Genesis of the Tree. There's a lot to lose here because we know there's even more to gain as the light concords the darkness. We personally know that our self-actualization can make something where there is nothing.

From our point of view, our thoughts are motions towards securing our survival and our family's survival.

We are extensions of the Tree's attempts to grow and survive. That's why our core priorities are family then self. That being true, all of our resolves and desires in life are oriented around and derived from the goals of the survival of the larger Tree of Life. These resolves and desires are coded into our DNA as basic reactionary systems and hormonal emotional systems. Our emotions are based off survival, breeding, and protecting family. That's what the Tree of Life needs.

From our internal perspective, our moment-to-moment interactions and behaviors are based off of what we refer to as fulfillment, which is emotionally based off family. This means that most if not all of our thoughts, behaviors, and emotions are oriented towards the opposite sex. That is why our life on Earth is a tight link between the two base forces of the masculine and the feminine. Life from our emotional standpoint is these two energies spinning around each other seeking to become one and resolve. Family and belonging are hidden goal and love is the answer.

All of our lives we dance with and around the opposite sex. Hopefully at some point we make a meaning full bridge into someone else's life, establish trust, and have children. Hopefully, we line it up right, know how to take care of that child, and teach it what it needs to survive. This is the motion of a person and a family surviving as individuals. From the bigger picture, you can see it's the motion of the Tree of Life growing and overcoming the inanimate space it found itself in. A place that was once without form, and void. A place where darkness was upon the face of the deep, but now there is light. It made that light. It made the light for us. It spreads, grows, and creates our experience as it steps through this place.

Dimorphic species have, at some point along the line, adapted a dual form approach to accelerating their genetic testing and adaptation processes. Species that have this dual form of genetic testing experience genetic recombination and acquire adaptations exponentially faster than species that have a monomorphic genetic alignment. Single form approach DNA must slowly achieve genetic recombination and slowly acquire adaptations through environmental or accidental means like radioactive genetic interference. These less predictable, environmental recombinations of the DNA are rarely stable and thus rarely produce a successful new genetic adaptation. They much more rarely create a DNA strain viable to recurring life. Monomorphic species evolve very slowly and stay stagnant when compared to dimorphic species.

Monomorphic genetic species are like genetic looping machines, and they just kind of run without much change. Dimorphic sexual selection is an advanced genetic adaptation strategy, and it's capable of extraordinary adaptation from generation to generation.

Dimorphic species, like humans, split their genetic configurations into two alignments, such as the human male and the human female. And those alignments are coded with hormonal sequences which produce emotional behavioral patterns that make the two forms seek each other emotionally for fulfillment. Our emotional/spiritual "seeking" is our individual energy of one of those two forms. The two forms of interacting energies are the masculine and feminine energy. The masculine and the feminine energy dance with each other and spin around each other in what I call "The Spiral." Emotionally speaking, the nature of our lives is a Spiral where the masculine and feminine spin around each other seeking to become whole. The world you see in front of you is a mask for that spiral motion. By mask, I mean that it looks like a bunch of small or large problems, but each of those problems is just an abstraction either physical or emotional to the pair bonding and family desires which are derived from the tension between the two base forces of the Spiral as it spins.

The two genetic forms in the dimorphic system have evolved to facilitate accelerated genetic adaptation. The two most notable hormones that highly differentiate the two forms are testosterone and estrogen. Males have more testosterone boosted from the point of egg fertilization on due to a section of genetic code inside the Y chromosome called the SRY component. In males, this testosterone boost starts at around two or three weeks of inception and produces exaggerated aggression, emotions of being a protector, physical lean muscle, and heavier bone density in general. Females lack a Y chromosome and ultimately have more estrogen. In females, this abundance of estrogen physically effects the fetus throughout development and produces stronger empathic emotions, accelerated abilities to read facial and tonal non-verbals, agreeableness, softer muscle tissue, and thinner bone density in general.

The testosterone washing over the male fetus from the Y chromosome produces accelerated features and exaggerates both physical and mental attributes which carries both the possibility of greatness and the possibility of utter failure. Male genetic outcomes are less stable and thus produces an experimental effect inside the two base forces. Female genetics are more stable and produce less variation which creates a stabilizing effect inside the two forces. This alignment of these two forces is what creates the accelerated genetic evolution of sexually dimorphic species.

One half is stable and the other is experimental. The stable half can consciously look across at the experimental half and make a breeding decision by choosing from the experiments that it sees on the other side. This is called sexual selection evolution. Unlike monomorphic species which must rely on radiation or long term accidental genetic recombination, dimorphic species experience a recombination every generation. The fertilized egg experiences a significant recombination. That genetic recombination is carried out with conscious intention. Sexually dimorphic species experience accelerated genetic adaptation fueled by oceans of unstable/experimental genetic patterns being observed and selected for breeding by an ocean of slightly more stable genetic patterns. The males are the experimental half and the females are the stable half.

This amazing hormonal balance is a miracle, and its genius. It facilitates both stability and broad experimentation of genetic combinations simultaneously. This is how humans have made it this far. The two forces are beautiful and have their purpose which we can only second guess to our demise. The Tree's plans are glorious. Our plans are ignorant, short sighted, and dangerous.

We have a lot of choices in life, and it seems like there's a lot to figure out. But in reality, we've been here for a long time, and we're more subject to the experience of life than the experience of life is to us. Some things are just written in the stars y'all. After all, there is no place like home. And you don't have to know why. It just is What It Is.

Lots of our problems are just perceived problems or problems with the way we are looking at things. We don't have to solve every problem, and the solution to most of the problems in our lives isn't a quest to march out into the world and solve, but instead the calm tranquility of simply moving in concert with our base imperative. This base imperative is simply going into the Spiral where our DNA contains emotional fulfillment for each of us. The path we seek in life isn't into the world but instead into the Spiral where we are elated by the Tree of Life instead of endlessly chasing our own ambition. The problems we see are masked discomforts based off genetic, hormonal signals that we are off the mark. We are either on the mark or off the mark. The mark, in the end, is actually the path that the Tree of Life is choosing. We are actually just choosing to move with the Tree of Life or in some other direction against the Tree of Life.

By choosing alternative paths, we find ourselves experiencing the emotions of sadness and loneliness which are actually hormones written into our DNA as signals of being off the path or off the mark. By choosing the path of the Tree of Life, we move in the direction of our genetic, hormonal, and emotional evolution and are biologically rewarded with fulfillment and elation hormones. Overall, the discontentment we feel in life is actually due to ignoring the Tree of Life and believing our own plan is better, which is a lie that we offer ourselves like a shiny apple from a snake. A snake that told us we can create something better than the garden we live in freely. By biting the apple, we only find out what fools we were to let go of the beautiful garden we had.

The path of fulfillment and long-term happiness is into our own minds to explore that hidden frontier with someone else that can go with you. Only a man and a woman can walk into this Spiral. The Spiral then produces offspring of yourself in which you can see a reflection of yourself and recognize it for the first time. Only though the Spiral can you find that you fulfilled your obligation to continue life and gave gratitude to the Tree of Life which brought you here.

There are many events that produce fulfillment along the right path of course. It's not as simple as just breeding. But the children are of course the key event along the path. Good examples, other than seeing your child born, are watching your daughter be married and carry on her own journey, watching your children's piano recitals, teaching your son how to ride a bike, seeing you daughter with her first child, etc. There are different stages of gifts from the Spiral like gifts from the early stages of dating and having kids vs. the gifts from the later stages of happiness like seeing your grandchildren grow, learn, and spending time with them. All of these are movements into the Spiral nature of life and revolve around your relationship with the opposite sex and building a strong bridge into the next generation for life.

When you see your daughter with her child, that is a movement into the Spiral and rewarding just like when you work on furniture with your grandson or go hunting. The Spiral nature of life is into the family orientation and teaching your offspring how to thrive in this world. The way to solve the world's perceived problems is not by seeking into the physical world, but instead by going into the Spiral because these listed activities produce contentment in all living beings.

Don't let anyone get in the way of your journey into the deeper realms of your experience, and don't think it's anyone else's job. Remember, the Tree of Life is testing the ground for fertile mentalities that can carry it on and, with that, has a vested interest in offering you death. That's why G-d made the snake. Never forget that G-d made that snake. The Tree of Life needs to find out if you're weak and dispatch you if you are. The only real dangers in our world are the disturbances in the Spiral nature of life, of which there are many. Your family is your responsibility and the world's problems are distractions that can work themselves out only when family and community become our focus. Don't fight the world. Just walk into the Spiral! It's what you were designed for and nothing else will work.

One last note, you have a purpose. This is not a coincidence. When you realize that you must confront the destiny you were given and what it will take to defend this Tree, you're going to have...

To Wake the Lion!

Origin Of Morality

Morality is thought sometimes to be socially derived. It seems more evolutionarily adaptive to me though. I find it apparent that the top of the hierarchy of needs is to understand What Is and finding purpose of spirit. Society can't get past a certain point without everyone understanding base morals and understanding fully what it means to be moral. This understanding can also not be forced. It must be realized internally through self-reflection after observation of the real world. We have to be observant enough to look at the world and derive what must be for us to continue generational growth.

Somehow our ancestors had a list with which to base a moral life. They align society and had values thousands of years before our time. These values turn out to be timeless and applicable in every generation and age. I'm talking about basic morals like not to steal and not to covet your neighbor's wife. What Is gave us those rules and told us we would never completely understand them but to follow them. By What Is, I mean The Thing That Is. The proper noun Thing That Is that denotes everything and our experience. The word God attempts this unfathomable denotation as well.

We live in a very masked society and we are constantly drawn away from discussing the things that would help us move forward. We are purposely dragged off the path. It's getting more difficult and almost impossible to say things that must be said to fix the growing mental illness around us. The world is officially very sick and it shows. Between political correctness and cultural Marxism, we are boxed in and the truth is boxed out. Only the brave will make it out. I'm here to rally the troops for what is to come. The truth is, we didn't create morality. It was shown to us to either accept or to deny. The world we thought we were in is fake and everyone is lying to you about almost everything. And worst of all, you are lying to yourself and trying to ignore it. We are officially part of the world's sickness.

Nietzsche said that people ignoring God, What Is, or What Is True would lead to people into thinking they must make their own reality and thus the rules of morality. He correctly noted that this would end in sorrow and nihilism. He was right about that of course. But given more time, I believe that Nietzsche would also come to the realization that this negative occurrence of a cycle of nihilism actually has a purpose. The prodigal son needed to go on his journey, right? It was his destiny and it is our destiny as well. The reason that it needs to happen is so that a species can see the degradation associated with moral collapse and human defined pseudo morals. Nihilism is a natural occurrence of a sickening species and a necessary internal reflection of an individual or species. This special point of internal reflection offers the golden opportunity to fully understand morality and its necessity in a way that is not forced. It's not forced on you because your revolt against the pseudo-morality of your fellow humans will start to tear into your mind and heart in a way that you will no longer be able to ignore. You're most likely near or at that point already. When you get there, you will know that we bring the sorrow upon ourselves. This is the only way to naturally prompt a push an individual and by proxy a species towards harmony in any society or species and Nietzsche seemed to miss that. The realization to not steal and covet is in our evolutionary path. It's not simply for the sake of being a good person.

Put more simply, people ignoring the basic commandments would lead to a time of nihilism sorrow and potential extinction. The reflection of the individuals at that point in time would forge a species that understood that we can't make our own morals and the commandments where the proper path, though they can't be proven. That's what I mean by the cycle of nihilism from which we learn and evolve. The tumultuous nature of our times is proof a golden opportunity is near.

Hard times produce good men. The good men are an evolutionary adaptation that is required to make it through that point in time. And, there will be more moral gates to our survival in the future assuming we come together and successfully pass through the current gate. Man-made pseudo morals bring about sorrow and death, while surrender to what has worked and base morals brings about thriving. It's a basic phenomenon in life, and we find that in time. God didn't die, we just stopped listening. But now we are dying, and we are starting to listen again. We have to and we will die if we don't. We don't choose what's moral and we never did.

The truth about it is that our commandments are not demands. They are offers of survival in a world that we could never tame with our bureaucracies and technology. And there would be no beauty in our worldly experience if you could not turn the commandments down. The world couldn't be beautiful if it couldn't be lost forever. There would be no beauty in What Is, The Thing That Is, if our survival and generations were guaranteed. The Thing That Is is fighting to be here and by proxy as a part of It, you are fighting to be here as well. It gave us the psychological and spiritual tools to accomplish this. They are the commandments.

Morality is not meant to be forced. This is what people are talking about when they say you can't legislate morals. If you could legislate morals then they wouldn't have any value and life would be solved without each person evolving. Morals are about the self-actualization of the individual and as it's said, can't be legislated or imposed. Life in time works towards harmony, that all beings will get along at a certain point, and they will live in a way that is sustainable for ages.

This is the end goal of the process of What Is, but What Is setup the equation so that we realize how we are to go about this on our own. It does not set it up to force you to behave. You can't force a horse to drink right. If you have to force the horse to drink, there's no value to the horse because it's going to be dead soon anyways. The only value in a horse is that it exists and knows to drink water on its own. Get ready for humanities great revival of faith, which we all see coming. Get ready for the shrieks from the ancient darkness that has held us back when you begin...

To Wake the Lion!

Why I Fight

I've been thinking a lot about what is fueling my most recent expansion into what I guess to be the eternal struggle. I've always been the type of person that stands up against some pretty specific types of injustices throughout my life. I'm far from perfect and I make a lot of mistakes. And I've accepted my imperfection, and with it a long time ago gave up worrying about my personal hypocrisy and not always doing the right thing. I've accepted my imperfection and I'm a very flawed person, but I feel more compelled than ever to stand strong against a specific set of injustices that I see unfortunately expanding in our world. To me, caring more about pushing back against these expanding injustices forces me to expand my resolve to push back against those injustices. And by forces, I mean that my mind is built in a way that I actually do not have a choice. I see something coming, and the very nature of my existence and every pillar of what I understand to be my purpose for existence is counter to standing by and watching the outrageous misfortune. I'm not saying that out of idealism. I'm specifically saying this because that inability is true of you too, and you are no doubt slowly coming to the realization that you can't just sit by and watch the world fall apart.

I, like all of you, see the turmoil in the world today. It's unavoidable. The perceived problems are numerous and each one most likely bigger than any of the individual problems that each one of us has faced before in our lives. I imagine that lots of people looking out into the landscape of our civilizations can't help but feel helpless. When I take a step back and look at it, I am in awe of how much pressure and stress humanity can endure and has endured. So, I am hopeful. I believe that while what I'm referring to here is a great darkness, we will prevail and life always finds a way.

This conversation is about me sorting out some of the reasons that I feel compelled to fight so hard against the dark injustices that I see. For some reason, I seem to take a much harder stance against these injustices than many of the people around me. I don't know why to tell you the truth, and it's a point of frustration for me. It's frustrating because I don't believe that I'm taking an irrationally hard stance with respect to the tragedy the world is becoming. I sincerely believe that others are not taking a strong enough stance against the injustices that they see, and our hiding is fueling the sorrow that's saturating our society.

I don't see many of the people fighting strongly or efficiently, but those that do are quickly becoming the heroes, protectors, and icons of our time. And those that are going along with the lies are quickly being identified as the villains and cowards of our time. The villains and cowards are in the open now as currently outnumber the heroes. But that's fine and expected. In a time when courage is so rare, courage is unmistakably visible and highly powerful. That's where we are. We are in a time of great deceit and little courage. People know exactly what I'm talking about and they can feel it around them. Cream rises to the top and the deceit of our time is starting to create a new generation of heroes that will move mountains by simply telling the truth. We are known for our deeds and not simply our words. It's my firm belief that the darkness comes when people don't speak their minds and cowards thrive.

The darkness, whatever you may be picturing when I say that, comes when our civilization becomes more of a series of accidental events. We as men and women are built to forge our destiny and do the things that we deem right for our communities and families. And though we make mistakes, like being imperfect, our civilization will work out what is right only when we are speaking up and defending ourselves and our integrity. That's why my fight is so important to me. When we don't speak our minds, we let the world slip. When we stop fighting for our families, children, grandchildren, and unborn, we are letting the world slip. We don't speak out for what is right when society starts to spoil and we fear the people around us not accepting our views. We let the world slip out of fear of ostracization or fear of retaliation.

There are of course reasons why people don't fight for themselves and those reasons are in ways rational. But our fears of retaliation are only rational to a point, and we are far past that point. I believe people know that we are far past the point of losing control inside of their own minds. The pressure from above and pressure from below puts them in a defensive mode where there frozen for the don't act or they just start moving into the darkness. The darkness is ultimately death and genocide of course but they don't know the answer is as simple as just speaking out and saying what is true.

It is no measure of sanity or safety to be well-adjusted to a sick society and the price of lying to oneself is indeed death. Honesty is our only salvation in this world. It's been shown in the greatest of examples that sacrifice and pain is required to preserve anything beautiful and we all have our cross to bear. Our voices are the light and that is ultimately much stronger than the darkness. I, and soon you, will not let the world slip into sleep and a series of accidental events. We will return this world and the human species back into a place where we make the decisions which were said to be the responsibility of the elusive professionals. We will return the world to the point of declaring what is right from wrong without fear of attack. We will do this for our families and the long-term greater human destiny.

Maybe I see the darkness more clearly than others, but I don't think so. Maybe I'm delusional and have simply spent too much time in some obscure echo chamber. Maybe I, through some experience's life, have simply made me more suitable to battle the misfortunes of the world. I can't answer lots of these questions, but I do feel that my vigor is not misguided. I naturally admit imperfection and revisit these types of questions in hopes of keeping myself in check. I have seen points in my life where I have failed to act and points where I over reacted. I make it a point to fight viciously against the injustices that I am seeing expanding over the world. I consider myself fierce and at times appropriately brutal. I do not believe this to be misguided and you shouldn't fear or avoid your passion.

I believe the world has lost its fighters and philosophers, but only temporarily. The darkness in the turmoil does tend to make heroes. The heroes of this upcoming era of oppression and sorrow are going to be nothing short of biblical grade champions. It's going to be an era of heroes who fight with their pens and lives in ways that we've only read about at rare moments in our history. At those points in history, we see true human greatness and the rare glowing spirit of courage that we are so drawn towards. The heroes of the coming era will live out long and glorious stories of the transformation back to a beautiful world. The beauty they fight for will only become visible as the world itself starts to slip in between our fingers.

I see a more beautiful world for all of us than what we were told was possible, and it's hiding just around the corner or our courage momentarily. Every one of us remembers better times, and everyone knows that we could have something unfathomably abundant. I see how beautiful the world can and will be now that it's slipping away, and I believe that we are spiritually and biologically programmed to love the world so much that we ultimately will give anything to preserve it. To preserve life. And make no mistake about the darkness; Life is it's enemy.

As pessimistic as some of this may sound, it's okay and I know you can see it too. We know that ignoring it is worse. I have faith that it's just a lesson for us, and it's a lesson whose time has come. The darkness is a natural phenomenon that comes when we stop compelling our will. Our will is to preserve life and our family. So quite naturally, when we stop expressing our will, life and our family stopped being expressed proportionately. We now no doubt all individually feel the stress of this in our individual lives. I see this stress in our lives as a symptom and the real problem is good people not speaking up for what is right. Viewing the world in this way creates a terror in me of not expressing myself. I'm not perfect and you are not perfect, but in general we will end up moving towards something peaceful and harmonious if left to our own conversations and concerns. The aggregate actions of humanity compel us towards basic respect for each other that stems directly from and is sociologically an extension of the love of our family and children. Our evolutionary path does compel us towards peace and harmony though there are hard lessons along the way.

It's all evolution of our minds, and the beautiful world that we are destined for is written in our DNA. I see it and the most amazing places. I see a more beautiful world inside of children's eyes as they play and explore before they've learned our adult problems. I see it and feel it whenever I observe a speaker, athlete, or hero of any sort self-actualize in front of me. And I see it in the eyes of the adults around me when they choose fight the outrageous misfortunes when they're not even guaranteed victory or survival.

That is why I fight with my pen as viciously as I can. We are no longer, and maybe we never were, in a time where we can go along quietly with what we see rotting around us. And the heroes are coming. The heroes are on their way. But you don't need to wait for them, because most likely, at some point, you are one of them. As the message gets less and less subtle, simply passing by will no longer suffice. The darkness leaves no stone unturned and it will come for you sooner than later. Even if you believe that you are simply playing it safe in a precarious time, ultimately the human spirit that lives in each one of us, and you, will realize that everything is at risk. Your spirit has most likely already noticed that what is slipping away is more valuable than your job, your social status, and material possessions. There comes a point when you will give up everything you have and you will gain everything else.

And though for each individual that time may be different, it's coming quicker and quicker every day now. Can't you feel the speed at which our society is being altered by the darkness. Can't you feel how people's very grip on reality is becoming hazy. Mental illness and immorality are metastasizing exponentially at this point. When the time comes for you to stop playing so safe and move towards what you know is better and right, you will feel the weight of our chains and the fear of the darkness lift off of you. When you choose to put the fear of ostracization behind you and in faith put everything you think you have on the line, you will accept that you will most likely lose everything you thought you had, including the security who you thought you were. That's the true fear inside of us. The fear of losing their station in life and security of what people around them currently think about them.

We fear people finding out that we don't have it all figured out. These fears are deep-seated, completely natural, protective psychology, and internally terrifying. We all face these most treacherous fears all alone in our heads. They are understandably scary but fortunately self-imposed paper tigers. They are not real. Every one of us in our own way passionately seeks to overcome what we falsely perceive as inabilities to express ourselves. Enter the hero, the person you really are.

The person that boldly rejects the coward. Isn't that your true adventure? An adventure that no one else knows you are on. The version of you that would shock your friends. It's definitely my adventure and the most exciting peril that I have ever experienced. Life's an adventure where we seek passion, and passion is always some form of expressing ourselves.

Watch the signs. Society is quickly being altered by darkness that is brought on by our fear of ostracization and fear of losing our station in life. This causes us to play through life's events safely in a tumultuous time in need of bold people. We are currently entering the greatest adventure in human history, and as the heroes show up, you will lose your fear of speaking up, and you will lose your fear of defending yourself and your way of life. As you start to see how beautiful this world can be, you will choose to take that scary step of put your finances, your job, and reputation on the line for that beautiful world you envision with your family. As you and the people around you do this, we will reestablish the order and general security in our world that we are now missing so much.

When you put this everything on the line, you will not fear losing that everything you thought you had because you will see what is being lost and what is to gain. When you take that scary step into the unknown and into faith, only then will all these stressors of the world that you feel expanding daily be lifted off of you. If you feel the weight against you in a grocery store, then you have to fight the darkness in the grocery store. If you feel the weight against you at work, then you have to fight the darkness in your place of work. There are no places where the darkness isn't intruding into your life, and nowhere is exempt from the battle.

The battle of life is against fake realities. Fake realities such as the constantly fraudulent news cycles, altered visions of what makes a healthy family, public education raising our children to be at odds with their own bloodlines and nations, and the glorification of sexuality over love and sexual responsibility. Common sense conversations with healthy minded people naturally dissolve all of these fake realities and we simply need to stand up and have those common-sense conversations again. Common sense and plain truth are the theme of the coming era which fights back the darkness by the heroes as they rise. And what an adventure. I'm so glad to be living in hard times like this where we have a chance to see the darkness and let it compel us to fight. We are lucky to live in a time where we will see the glorious rise the most prolific heroes that are DNA can achieve. I've seen the beauty in life and I want more.

    I want to thank each and every one of you for being strong this life and being in this life with me. I want to thank you for the contributions you have made and will make towards bringing order back to the world. It's an adventure and yes, it's going to be epic. It won't be an easy adventure though hero, and you are going to have…

To Wake the Lion!

The Power of Self-Actualization

In today's world, we have more options for media and communication than ever before in history. Each one of us use a variety of web sites, news, sources, and media channels to follow a list of people who we feel add value to our lives with their words and views. We also tend to gravitate towards people in our personal life that compel interesting conversation and interaction. I've noticed a theme to the people that I am most interested in and the people that I keep around me.

The people I find interesting consistently speak outside of the mainstream social norm. They can tell when people are lying to themselves and take risks to preserve the truth. They are not afraid of the people around them, and they speak their minds freely. These people walk with a purpose because they have a purpose. People who do not fit in this theme seem inconsequential to life in general and appropriately fade into the background. These people are simply background characters in other people's lives.

I have spent some time thinking about the plight of the people that interest me. There is a common theme to their approaches to life and I think I've figured out what makes them act the way that they do. I've figured out what it is about them that I feel so gravitated towards. They seem to be digging deeper within themselves and fighting to self-actualize. They are fighting for something better within themselves and the world. As a greater human destiny becomes clearer to an individual, that vision becomes more powerful to them than the mainstream societal narrative. They then become unable to go with the flow. Simply passing by will no longer suffice. They wake up.

They are self-actualizing and there is nothing more interesting. Self-actualization is commonly thought of as the realization of one's potential, and the full development of one's abilities and appreciation for life. The push to self-actualize seems to compel a person's need for something better in the world and that need prevents them from being weak or mundane. A waking person stands out. We innately recognize them as the underdog in an ancient battle that has eaten and forgotten almost every man since Adam. On the deepest level, we root for them.

We naturally seek these people especially in time of turmoil and chaos when we are needing answers.

Becoming what we are supposed to become is the most significant part of our internal drive. Watching a person struggle to express themselves activates the deepest form of identification and bond between humans because we ourselves seek to express. We are built that way. We say that we are interested in people like this, however under the hood, we are drawn to their boldness to rise above the storm because we dream of a self that will rise above that same storm.

Inside our own minds and secretly in our own way we privately strive to make sense out the world that we are in, but not of. We seek to become something else. And we mostly don't know what it is that we want to become. It's something we can't put into words, but we know it's something greater than the complacent person that we have this far found ourselves as.

People are actually obsessed with the need to become; to self-actualize. It's what drives people to listen and be interested in the things that other people say. To express our thoughts and actualize our purpose are built into our struggles. Ultimately it is the struggle. We are starved for it. People go for months without hearing something that really touches them. Some people go for years. As the world spirals, people become distraught looking for fulfillment. Man does not live on bread alone. Material things run dry, and we need something else to build inner structure.

We slowly but surely find that we have to actualize our purpose. Our deeper resolutions are paramount in ways that we recognize more as the world starts to weigh on us. When you talk to people about something that really creates inner structure outside of the mainstream narrative, they recognize the tone of the conversation and begin to see you as real person. They begin to identify their deepest struggles with your attempts to connect with them. I see that people will make overtures to bridge the gap in your attempt in order to be a part of the expression and actualization you are attempting. It's what they wanted anyways. It's the binding aspect of our minds and the essence of interpersonal identification. We are often unknowingly pulled towards seeing and hearing a person self-actualizing into something greater. It's what we seek in the depths of our minds and like a campfire, everyone is drawn in and must stare. Recognize that it's what your interactions want and take a chance on saying something beautiful to someone today.

The most interesting people talk about becoming what they know they should be; self-actualization. For instance, when people talk about events in their life where they experienced something life altering. A point at which they were altered. We want to hear about people changing into something greater and the off chance that the events came about against all odds.

An interesting conversation tends to happen when a person shares something that is deeper and speaks to the inner most aspect of the self. People listen to those who address that inner journey and provide inspiration on that path. Be brave and show others the path outside of the social norms that hold us down. Show them that it's safe to walk out of the dark cave of social construction. Self-actualization must exist out of the social norm, and interesting people always seem beyond the arbitrary social limitations of the day. Throughout history and also today, the enemies of the inner-self have always been the gatekeepers of the mainstream narrative. The gatekeepers are usual suspects like the mainstream media and the collectivists of the day.

Only dead fish swim with the current. History forgets the weak, the capitulators, and those who fear the gatekeeps. The present often forgets them as well. Respect is reserved for those bold enough to take a risk and speak truth in the empire of lies. The bold particularly command our respect because the bold will put something on the line and take the risk to express what needs to be expressed to become something greater. Weak people capitulate because they have no greater vision for their world. They lack the self-respect required to change the fate the gatekeepers have assigned them. The gatekeepers are the manufacturers of fear and the harvesters of sorrow.

The brave know that they risk what they have if they are to become something greater. They have self-respect and with that are dissatisfied with anything less than the greater human destiny they envision. Their inner power is alluring on a whole other level and unmistakable. That is the power of expression. It's our super power of self-actualization and inside each soul.

Be that person. Be the lion. Don't be the boring person you portray to others. Say something you're not supposed to say to. Say something true. Let others around you see what it looks like to put something on the line and take a risk. Only those people who have something to lose can be bold enough to offer it to others. Only those seeking the deepest and most exhilarating adventure can offer that adventure to others.

As sure as bold people are rare, the most interesting thing about a person is their self-actualization. When people notice it, it's impossible to ignore and people recognize the rarity of that boldness. If you want to see what's outside the box, you must first get out of the box. Be your bold alter ego because that's actually who you are. But if you're going to become who you really are, you going to have...

To Wake the Lion!

Why I Write

I write for several reasons, and I've reasoned on it for a while now. I think I've come up with a decent set of my driving factors which you may find interesting.

I have a need for to write, which is interesting because I'm not a good writer as you may notice. I'm ok with that now. I've adopted it as a style, and I'll blame the rest on artistic license. Importantly though, I suspect it may be more useful to some people to read a non-writer's words as opposed to the words of the greats. Maybe it's an insight into our need for self-expression from a someone who shouldn't be writing. I'm in route to say what I need to say without fear of imperfection. I'm not perfect. That's the human condition, and I'm happily a part of it.

I write to help sort out my thoughts. Everything is happening so fast these days. Writing helps rest my nerves which are on fire from outrageous misfortune. I base a lot of my writing off aspects of the world that I feel society pushes against us figuring out. I feel like I'm doing my part by helping open the conversations that solve our deeper problems. The misfortunate aspects of our society that build into outrage are all the same as they have ever been. Old tricks are the best tricks. Nothing really ever changes, and the wise fight back the darkness by bringing the same lessons to the people of their time. That is our job as thinkers.

I feel writing helps me clear the muddy water of our confusing world. I get nervous when the waters get too muddy, and now is definitely time. If you feel like the world is too complicated, you may feel better to write and share your thoughts. Maybe you will enjoy some part of my writings and would be encouraged to join the fight. The pen is mightier than the sword. Simple people are the ones who write the most daring or intriguing thoughts in the end. Who cares what the professionals write? Who cares what the elite write? The meek are the real power in this world. If you like the way that sounds, then pick up the pen.

Aside from our salvation and disbanding the outrageous misfortune, I write because I feel like we very confused about something important. I don't know exactly what that important thing is, but I can feel it. We are not whole. I'm perpetually bothered by it. I have always felt that the mainstream projected world wasn't real. I feel if I can say the truest thing possible then I will have created something truly beautiful in the face of great confusion and impossible odds.

Isn't that what the real tragedy of life and source of our fears? Our inability to show others what is on our minds or what we see. The tragedy of knowing we are separate. I plan to say something beautiful and raw with compassion. Whatever it turns out to be.

I want to say something true that people feel or recognize. Something which is so simply true that it's been forgotten in the storm of the outer world. Something we all seek unknowingly that we can feel striking into our hearts when someone gets close to saying it. Whatever it may be.

My thought articles are that and nothing more. The tiny truths we operate on subconsciously get masked by our fears and social obligations. I feel that stepping through my fear by diving into the deep is the ultimate form of compassion and care for others. Honesty is the basis of respect for others. Honesty with one's self is the basis of self-respect and the trajectory of the truly adventurous.

The last reason I'll mention that I write is something that I've alluded to in the beginning of this thought. I want to show others that self-expression is paramount and expression is imperfect like us. Equally important to the well thought out things we can safely be sure of are the things we can't work out easily that still must be said. Conversation will be set free.

The deepest things are impossible for us to accurately reason on, and that makes our journey spiral towards being ok with our humanistic attempts at the bold. We seek self-expression as our destiny and the spice of life. Our resolve is contestant and paramount. There is always a new world to explore just one conversation away.

Thank you for reading and thank you for being a part of my journey! If you think this was at all interesting, give me some feedback. Like and subscribe. And don't forget...

To Wake the Lion!

Be Brave!

> Let them hear the breath of life.
>
> It's time.
>
> Wake the Lion.

www.ingramcontent.com/pod-product-compliance
Lightning Source LLC
Chambersburg PA
CBHW060404080526
44583CB00012B/470